A TRUE BOOK

Extreme Places
The Wettest and the Driest

KATIE MARSICO

Children's Press®
An Imprint of Scholastic Inc.

Content Consultant
Injeong Jo, PhD
Assistant Professor
Department of Geography
Texas State University
San Marcos, Texas

Library of Congress Cataloging-in-Publication Data
Marsico, Katie, 1980– author.
The wettest and the driest / by Katie Marsico.
  pages cm. — (A true book)
  Summary: "Learn all about the wettest and driest places on Earth and find out what it takes for life to survive in these extreme locations." — Provided by publisher.
  ISBN 978-0-531-21847-1 (library binding : alk. paper) — ISBN 978-0-531-21786-3 (pbk. : alk. paper)
  1. Extreme environments—Juvenile literature. 2. Floods—Juvenile literature. 3. Droughts—Juvenile literature. 4. Meghalaya (India)—Juvenile literature. 5. Atacama Desert (Chile)—Juvenile literature. I. Title. II. Series: True book.
  GB58.M377 2016
  551.6—dc23   2015009986

All rights reserved. Published in 2016 by Children's Press, an imprint of Scholastic Inc.
Printed in the United States of America 113
SCHOLASTIC, CHILDREN'S PRESS, A TRUE BOOK™, and associated logos are trademarks and/or registered trademarks of Scholastic Inc.
1 2 3 4 5 6 7 8 9 10 R 25 24 23 22 21 20 19 18 17 16

Front cover (main): A sandboarder on a sand dune

Front cover (inset): Waterfalls in Croatia's Plitvička Lakes National Park

Back cover: Workers wearing Khasi umbrellas in Mawsynram, India

Find the Truth!

Everything you are about to read is true *except* for one of the sentences on this page.

Which one is **TRUE**?

T or F   There are no bridges in Meghalaya because lumber quickly rots in the soggy climate.

T or F   Droughts sometimes cause widespread starvation.

Find the answers in this book.

Contents

**Congo African
gray parrot**

THE **BIG** TRUTH!

Awesome Adaptations

How have animals adapted to their
extreme wet and dry environments? . . **26**

4

Extreme floods have affected people around the world.

4 Drenched by Natural Disaster

5 A Deadly Dry Spell

The rare candelabro cactus is native only to the desert regions of Peru and Chile.

5

Meghalaya receives more than 16 times the average annual U.S. rainfall.

CHAPTER **1**

From Drenched to Bone Dry

Residents of Meghalaya (may-guh-LAY-uh), a state in northeastern India, are used to heavy rains soaking the lush landscape around them. Meghalaya is known as the "wettest place on Earth." The state receives 467 inches (1,186 centimeters) of rainfall a year. People there often wear special waterproof *knups* over their head and back. Much like hands-free umbrellas, knups allow residents of Meghalaya to farm and work outdoors despite the extremely soggy climate.

Extreme Climates

Meghalaya is an example of an area with an extreme climate. Yet not all climate extremes involve heavy **precipitation**. Some are defined by extreme dryness. In portions of the Atacama Desert in South America, not a single drop of rain has ever been recorded. Nevertheless, more than 1 million people have found ways to **adapt** to life in this bone-dry land.

Many people raise animals such as llamas in parts of the Atacama where hardy scrubs and grasses manage to grow.

Children in Truni, Indonesia, travel to school by boat during a period of severe flooding.

Extreme Events

Extreme wetness and extreme dryness can also be the result of severe weather. Floods are generally the result of heavy rain or snow causing a body of water to rise and overflow. **Droughts** occur when an area experiences an unusually long period of little or no rainfall. Such extreme events affect everything from geography to agriculture. In many cases, floods and droughts also cause extensive property damage, injury, and death.

Certain species of animals, such as the Fabian's lizard, are found only in the Atacama desert.

Adapting to the Environment

In some situations, precipitation extremes challenge the survival and growth of any form of life. Nevertheless, people, plants, and animals have been known to overcome these challenges. Over time, they have developed adaptations to extreme wetness and dryness. For plants and animals, adaptations take the form of physical traits that help them tolerate precipitation extremes.

Humans have often used technology to adapt to extreme wetness and dryness. For instance, scientists set up weather stations to track local precipitation. With the help of engineers and government officials, they have developed methods to combat the effects of floods and droughts. Along the way, people have become more knowledgeable about the incredible—and sometimes dangerous—extremes of wetness and dryness that shape their environment.

Sandbags are sometimes added to protective structures to help reinforce them against flooding.

The city of Mawsynram in Meghalaya receives roughly 13 times as much rainfall as Seattle, Washington.

CHAPTER 2

A Rare, Rain-Soaked World

What makes the wettest place on earth so wet? A large part of the answer has to do with Meghalaya's geography. Southwest of this state in India lies a series of **floodplains** in the nearby nation of Bangladesh. In summer, air currents move north across the floodplains and collect moisture along the way. The currents eventually reach Meghalaya, which is filled with steep hills.

Meghalaya, India

Keeping in the Rain

The air currents must travel high into the atmosphere to pass over the hills. In the cold, thin air at these high elevations, the moisture in the currents condenses and collects in clouds above the hills. These clouds grow until they cannot hold any more moisture, releasing it as precipitation.

This leads to the constant, heavy rains that soak Meghalaya in summer. This climate pattern has fueled the development of the region's lush rain forests.

Dense rain forests cover Meghalaya's Khasi Hills.

An insect perches on the edge of a pitcher plant.

Lush Life

Meghalaya's **tropical** landscape is home to a rich variety of animal and plant life. Tigers, gibbons, and birds such as hornbills and eagles make their homes there. Unusual Indian pitcher plants are carnivorous, or meat eating. They trap insects with a specialized pitcher-shaped pouch.

The warm, moist environment fuels the state's main source of income: farming. Residents grow tea, corn, ginger, oranges, and many other foods. Rice thrives in the wet rice paddies of the region.

Bamboo is often used as a skeleton to guide rubber tree roots into forming a bridge.

Built to Withstand the Wetness

In some cases, residents of Meghalaya rely on local plant life to help them adapt to their soggy surroundings. For example, the area is known for its "living bridges." These bridges, which stretch across Meghalaya's valleys, are constructed from the sprawling roots of living rubber trees. Builders create the bridges by guiding young roots in desired directions, so they grow around or through other pieces of wood.

Building material such as lumber rots quickly due to the region's extreme wetness. In contrast, living bridges may last more than 500 years! The roots of Meghalaya's rubber trees grow as time passes. The bridges become stronger as they get older.

Despite their successful adaptations, residents of Meghalaya face serious challenges. Rains are heaviest between May and September. During these months, potentially deadly floods and mudslides are common occurrences.

Parents rescue their child from the roof of their home during a flood.

Ollague Volcano rises above the Atacama Desert in northeastern Chile.

Plant, animal, and human life is sparse in the Atacama Desert.

CHAPTER 3

Little to No Rainfall

While sheets of rain pound the hilltops of Meghalaya, not a drop drips onto the parched sand of the Atacama Desert. The Atacama stretches roughly 600 miles (966 kilometers) from Peru's southern border into Chile, Bolivia, and Argentina. On average, much of the desert receives less than 0.04 inches (1 millimeter) of rain a year. In contrast, Death Valley in the United States receives as much as 2 inches (51 mm) a year. In some areas of the Atacama, it is not unusual for absolutely no rain to fall.

Atacama Desert

Why So Dry?

The extreme dryness of the Atacama is tied to its geography. A large portion of the desert sprawls into the western Andes Mountains. Pressure from the atmosphere pushes air from higher mountain elevations down toward the ground below. However, this air releases hardly any moisture. The result is little to no rainfall over the Atacama.

A rhea, a relative of the emu and ostrich, walks in the Atacama Desert near the Andes.

Rain forests cover Peru's Urubamba Valley in the Andes mountain range.

Here is why that air is so dry: Warm, moist air blows in from the east and regularly soaks South America's rain forests. Upon reaching the eastern side of the Andes, however, the cold air high in the mountains causes it to cool. The air then releases its moisture over the mountains in the form of rain or snow. As it moves down the other side of the Andes, the air warms up again. However, at this point it contains hardly any moisture and is unlikely to produce rain in the desert.

Plants such as the candelabro cactus grow very slowly in the dry Atacama Desert.

Not Lacking Life

Some parts of the Atacama are so dry that they do not appear to support any form of life. In other areas, however, plants and animals have adapted to the lack of precipitation. For example, certain cacti and shrubs have extremely far-reaching roots (see page 25). This feature allows them to drain underground water sources that may be several feet away.

Flamingos are sometimes spotted in the Atacama. These birds are usually seen near the desert's salt lakes. Such lakes once held more water but gradually began to dry up. The water that remains is filled with large amounts of salt. **Algae** grow in the Atacama's salt lakes and provide food for flamingos and other local animals.

A flock of flamingos fills a lake in the Andes.

Other Ways of Getting Water

People have also learned how to survive—and even to farm—in the Atacama. Some residents use **aquifers** to water their land. Others rely on small streams formed by melting snow in the mountains.

More farmers are also beginning to investigate fog catchers. These mesh nets are supported by pipes. The mesh traps **vapor** when fog drifts into the Atacama. The vapor turns into water droplets that drip down the pipes into collection tanks.

Fog catchers are being used in many places across South America.

24

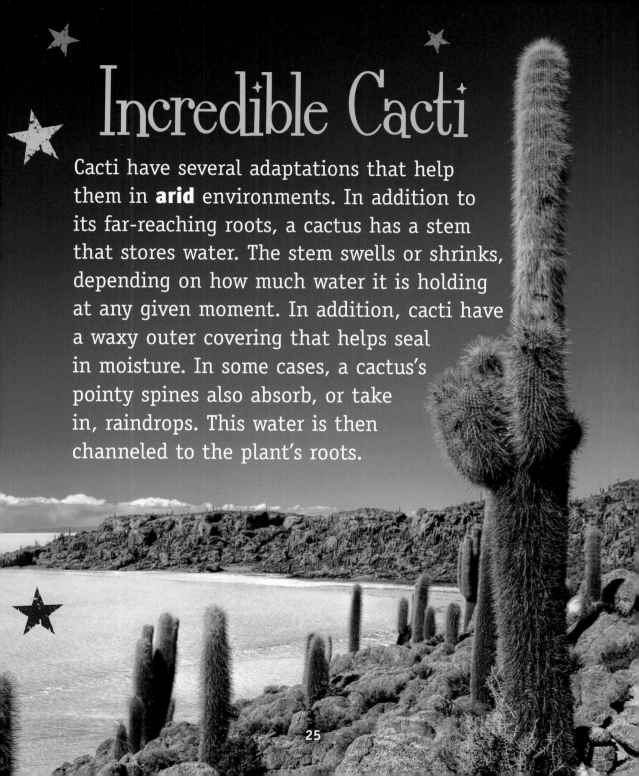

Incredible Cacti

Cacti have several adaptations that help them in **arid** environments. In addition to its far-reaching roots, a cactus has a stem that stores water. The stem swells or shrinks, depending on how much water it is holding at any given moment. In addition, cacti have a waxy outer covering that helps seal in moisture. In some cases, a cactus's pointy spines also absorb, or take in, raindrops. This water is then channeled to the plant's roots.

Awesome Adaptations

Both extreme wetness and extreme dryness can make it difficult to survive. Nonetheless, rain forests and deserts alike are home to a wide variety of unique animals. These creatures' amazing adaptations help them endure the challenges of their environments.

Powdered Parrots

In rain forests, extreme wetness is a way of life. Wet feathers tend to make flying difficult for birds. However, tropical birds such as Congo African gray parrots have special "powder down feathers" that produce a fine dust. The dust creates a waterproofing effect that prevents the birds from becoming soaked.

Shrimp Survival

In Australia's desert regions, shield shrimp live a short yet productive life. They hatch from eggs in puddles and lakes that form during brief rainy periods. The shrimp live only a few weeks but lay more hard-shelled eggs before dying. When the puddles dry up, winds blow these eggs across the desert. During the next rainy spell, new generations of shield shrimp hatch!

Floating Fire Ants

Fire ants are often found in grasslands or damp wooded areas. Sometimes these locations flood. To survive, fire ants cling to one another to form a type of living raft. Water does not seep inside the insects' tight-knit formation, which allows them to stay afloat. If necessary, fire ants can remain adrift for weeks!

Rodents That Recycle

Kangaroo rats live in dry desert regions throughout the western and southwestern United States. Within their cool underground burrows, the rodents' breath condenses, or changes from gas particles to liquid. The dry seeds that kangaroo rats store inside their burrows soak up these droplets of moisture. When the rodents eventually eat the seeds, they also get recycled water.

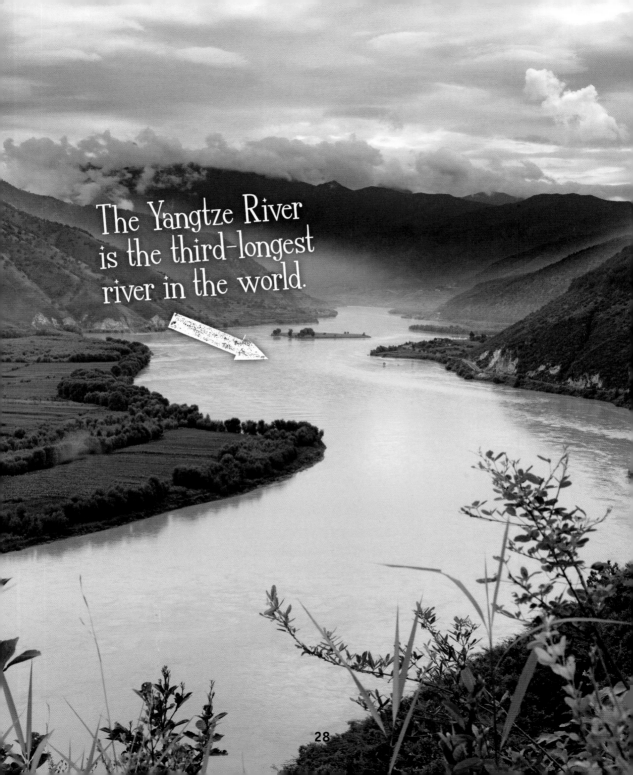

The Yangtze River is the third-longest river in the world.

CHAPTER 4

Drenched by Natural Disaster

A look at the super-dry Atacama climate shows how precipitation extremes can become part of people's day-to-day lives. In extreme weather events, however, precipitation during a short period can forever change life as people know it. For example, in 1931, heavy rains unleashed a devastating flood along China's Yangtze River. With many people and farms located in the densely populated region, the flood proved to be among the worst natural disasters of the 20th century.

Yangtze River

People shop at a flooded market in Hankou, China, in 1931.

When the Waters Rose

As early as 1930, people in China were dealing with more precipitation than usual. That winter, there was more snowfall than normal. The following spring and summer, extremely heavy rains fell. Both of these weather patterns caused the Yangtze River—which runs through much of China—to swell. On August 18, 1931, the river peaked and overflowed onto the land around it.

The Yangtze flooded 500 square miles (1,295 sq km) of land. In August alone, roughly 500,000 people fled their homes to escape to higher ground. To make matters worse, the skies did not show any signs of clearing. Continued rainfall drenched local rice farms. Much of that year's crop was destroyed, and starvation became a serious threat. In addition, the polluted river led to the spread of often deadly diseases.

The 1931 floods affected roughly one-fourth of China's population at the time.

The floodwaters reached a peak of 53 feet (16 meters) in the summer of 1931. Yet flooding continued to soak much of the land along the Yangtze for months. The disaster affected roughly 51 million people. An estimated 3.7 million individuals drowned or died due to starvation or disease.

The Top 10 Deadliest Floods*

Rank	Year	Location	Total Deaths
#1	1931	China	As many as 3.7 million
#2	1887	China	As many as 2 million
#3	1938	China	As many as 700,000
#4	1975	China	210,000
#5	1935	China	145,000
#6	1530	The Netherlands	More than 100,000
#7	1971	North Vietnam	100,000
#8	1911	China	As many as 100,000
#9	1287	The Netherlands	As many as 80,000
#10	1212	The Netherlands	60,000

*Why are China and the Netherlands so heavily represented in this chart? China's dense population make flooding along its two longest rivers particularly deadly. In the Netherlands, some coastal areas are below sea level, leaving them especially prone to flooding from the sea.

Volunteers and police officers in New Orleans, Louisiana, transport people to safety during the floods caused by Hurricane Katrina in 2005.

Learning From Fatal Floods

Other floods have affected China and many other countries throughout the world since 1931. Unfortunately, extreme precipitation still often leads to both property damage and death. Yet, after flooding occurs, scientists, engineers, and community leaders study what happened. Their work paves the way for better methods of avoiding and addressing future floods.

Engineers redesigned and rebuilt levees in New Orleans after the city's levee system failed under the force of Hurricane Katrina.

Protection and Preparation

Efforts to better control floodwaters sometimes involve building stronger dams and **levees**. These structures are built along rivers or other bodies of water. They block or redirect the water to prevent flooding or protect farmland. In other cases, experts suggest planting more trees in areas at risk of flooding. The tree roots create tiny spaces between particles of soil. When it rains, water drains into these spaces rather than into already swollen streams and rivers.

Scientists also prepare for extreme precipitation by carefully monitoring weather conditions. Technology has advanced a great deal since 1931. As a result, **meteorologists** can use satellites, computers, and the media to predict, track, and communicate weather patterns. This allows for more advanced warning if flooding is likely. With adequate warning, people have a better chance of protecting their property. Most importantly, they can evacuate, or leave the area, if necessary.

Meteorologists carefully track hurricanes and other storm systems to help people prepare for natural disasters.

35

China continues to face periods of drought today.

In China, natural disasters affect 200 million people yearly.

A Deadly Dry Spell

Between 1876 and 1879, China faced a different weather extreme. This time, floodwaters were the least of people's worries. For three years, the Chinese suffered one of the deadliest droughts in world history. By 1879, as many as 13 million lives had been lost due to this dangerous and unforgettable dry spell.

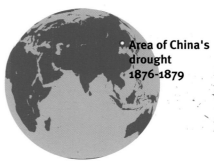

Area of China's drought 1876-1879

Poverty, Starvation, and Sickness

Starting in the summer of 1876, little to no rain fell over much of northern China. Nearly 150 years later, experts continue to debate what caused this lack of precipitation. What has been far clearer are the consequences of this extreme dryness. As time passed, water levels in rivers, lakes, and streams fell dramatically. In some cases, the bodies of water dried up altogether.

Droughts severely damage crops, such as these tobacco plants in southwestern China.

The Top 10 Deadliest Droughts*

Rank	Year	Location	Total Deaths
#1	1876–1879	China	13 million
#2	1932–1934	Soviet Union	As many as 10 million
#3	1936	China	5 million
#4	1921–1922	Soviet Union	As many as 5 million
#5	1928–1930	China	3 million
#6	1900	India	As many as 3 million
#7	1941	China	2.5 million
#8	1943	Bangladesh	1.9 million
#9	1965–1967	India	At least 1.5 million
#10	1943	Sudan	1.5 million

*Records of droughts that occurred before the mid-19th century are often too incomplete or inaccurate to be reliably compared to more recent events.

As the water disappeared, plants started to wither and die. This drove up the price on the limited number of crops that managed to survive. By 1879, poverty and starvation had torn apart or completely destroyed millions of lives. People ate grass and dirt out of desperation, but it usually did little good. Weak and lacking fresh water, they also suffered from a wide variety of diseases that spread easily.

California has suffered severe droughts in the 2010s.

In 1878, rainfall fiinally put an end to the extreme dryness in some portions of northern China. In other areas, it was not until 1879 that the long-awaited rains returned. Even then, it took time for survivors to regain their health and rebuild their lives. Today, droughts continue to affect people around the globe. The length of time they last and the destruction they cause varies. However, they are still often devastating.

Dealing With Droughts

As with floods, people are constantly trying to find new and better ways of dealing with droughts. For instance, meteorologists make the public aware of weather patterns that may signal extreme dry spells. In addition, people have developed techniques that help lessen the impact of little to no precipitation. Improved **irrigation** systems and collecting rainwater are just a couple of examples.

Students in Bukwo, Uganda, wash their hands with water collected from a building's roof.

Flooding the Fields

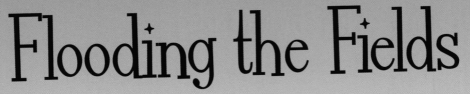

Rice is a major part of the diet of about half of all people on Earth. It is also a thirsty plant. The crop generally grows in large fields, or paddies, that remain flooded throughout the growing season. Even rice paddies in rainy regions or along rivers can—and do—face water shortages. In response, many farmers are adopting a new way of watering called Alternate Wet and Dry (AWD) irrigation. In AWD, the paddy dries until the water falls to 6 inches (15 cm) below the surface of the soil. Rice roots can still reach the water, so no crops are lost. The field is then flooded and allowed to dry again.

A flooded rice field

Huge amounts of rain support South America's Amazon River and connected rivers, which form the largest river basin in the world.

Amazing Extremes

Floods and droughts reflect the dangers of extreme precipitation and extreme dryness. Yet these extremes are often just as dazzling as they are destructive. Proof lies in the lush, green hilltops of Meghalaya and in the bone-dry but stunning Atacama. From humid rain forests and arid deserts to overwhelming floods and droughts, extremes help shape the world. And, time and again, people and other organisms demonstrate their ability to adapt to these powerful forces. ★

Annual rainfall in Meghalaya, India: 467 in. (1,186 cm)

Meghalaya's annual rainy season: May to September

Population of the Atacama Desert: More than 1 million people

Annual rainfall in much of the Atacama: Less than 0.04 in. (1 mm)

Height floodwaters reached in China in 1931: 53 ft. (16 m)

Number of deaths that resulted from China's 1931 flood: About 3.7 million

Number of deaths that resulted from China's 1876–1879 drought: As many as 13 million

Did you find the truth?

F There are no bridges in Meghalaya because lumber quickly rots in the soggy climate.

T Droughts sometimes cause widespread starvation.

Resources

Books

Arlon, Penelope, and Tory Gordon-Harris. *Rainforest*. New York: Scholastic, 2013.

Benoit, Peter. *Hurricane Katrina*. New York: Children's Press, 2012.

Eagen, Rachel. *Flood and Monsoon Alert!*. Crabtree Publishing, 2011.

Gerber, Larry. *Adapting to Droughts*. New York: Rosen Publishing, 2013.

Peppas, Lynn. *The Atacama Desert*. New York: Crabtree Publishing Company, 2013.

Visit this Scholastic Web site for more information on wettest and driest places:
★ www.factsfornow.scholastic.com
Enter the keywords **Wettest and Driest**

Important Words

adapt (uh-DAPT) — to change over time to fit in better with the environment

algae (AL-jee) — small plants without roots or stems that grow in water

aquifers (AH-kwuh-fuhrz) — underground layers of rock, sand, gravel, or silt that contain or conduct water

arid (AR-id) — extremely dry due to lack of rain

droughts (DROUTS) — long periods of time without rain

floodplains (FLUHD-playnz) — nearly flat areas that are located near streams or rivers and often prone to flooding

irrigation (ir-uh-GAY-shuhn) — supplying water to crops by man-made means, such as channels and pipes

levees (LEV-eez) — banks built up near a river to prevent flooding

meteorologists (mee-tee-uh-RAH-luh-jists) — scientists who study Earth's atmosphere and weather patterns

precipitation (pri-sip-i-TAY-shuhn) — water that falls from the sky in the form of rain, snow, sleet, or hail

tropical (TRAH-pi-kuhl) — of or having to do with the hot, rainy area of Earth near the equator

vapor (VAY-pur) — a gas formed from something that is usually a liquid or solid at normal temperatures

Index

Page numbers in **bold** indicate illustrations.

About the Author

Katie Marsico graduated from Northwestern University and worked as an editor in reference publishing before she began writing in 2006. Since that time, she has published more than 200 titles for children and young adults. Ms. Marsico enjoyed learning about precipitation extremes and would love to visit both Meghalaya and the Atacama one day.

The Wettest and the Driest

Where is the wettest place on Earth?

Meghalaya, a state in northeastern India. It receives around 467 inches (1,186 centimeters) of rain every year.

INSIDE, YOU'LL FIND:

★ What effects a severe drought can have on an area;

★ A timeline, photos—and why floods can be so devastating;

★ Surprising TRUE facts that will shock and amaze you!

ALL NEW ALL TRUE!

ISBN: 978-0-531-2178

Children's Press®
an imprint of

SCHOLASTIC

www.scholastic.com/librarypublishing

U.S. $6.95